Egyptian Rice Cooked in a Clay Bram

INGREDIENTS

3 cups whole milk

1 teaspoon sea salt

2 egg yolks

1 1/2 cups short-grain rice

(Paella rice, Arborio or even sushi rice would work)

3 tablespoons unsalted butter

DIRECTIONS

Preheat the oven to 385 degrees F.

Whisk together the milk, salt and egg yolks.

Combine the rice and milk mixture in a medium clay Bram or 4-quart Dutch oven.

Distribute the butter in thin shavings over the surface.

Place the Bram on a baking sheet as a safeguard from spills.

Cover with foil and bake for 30 minutes.

Uncover and bake until a rich, golden brown crust has formed on the top

And perimeter of the rice,

About 1 hour more. Most of the milk should have been absorbed.

Allow to sit at room temperature for 10 minutes before serving.

Egyptian Liver
Ingredients

1 lb beef liver

4 garlic cloves

3 teaspoons cumin powder

2 teaspoons ground coriander

2 teaspoons salt

1 teaspoon chili powder

3 green chilies

1⁄4 cup vegetable oil

3 limes, juice of

Directions

Chop up liver into small pieces.

Combine garlic, cumin powder, ground coriander, salt, chili powder and green chilies

In a food processor until they form a paste.

Add the mixture to the liver and let it sit for 15 minutes.

In a medium pan heat the oil and add the liver a little bit at a time

add the lime juice and cook for 15 minutes

CABBAGE ROLLS STUFFED WITH SPICED RICE (MAHSHI)
Ingredients

2 cups rice

1 head of cabbage (You will not be using all of it)

2 Tbsp Extra Virgin Olive Oil for rice

2 or 3 cups of Homemade Chicken/Vegetable Stock

(Or dissolve 1.5 bouillon cubes into 3 cups of hot water with some cumin

, cardamom seeds and black pepper for the same effect)

Herbs

1/2 bunch fresh parsley

1/2 bunch fresh dill, 1/2 bunch fresh cilantro

3 stalks of fresh mint leaves

Tomato Sauce

1/3 medium onion – minced

1 clove garlic – minced

1 ripe tomato – diced

1 can (5.5 Oz) tomato paste

2 Tbsp Extra Virgin Olive Oil

Salt and pepper to taste

Spice Mixture for Rice

2 teaspoons cumin

2 teaspoons black pepper

2 teaspoons cinnamon

2 teaspoons ground coriander

2 teaspoons paprika

1 teaspoon chili powder

1 teaspoon nutmeg

4-6 cardamom pods

Directions

Cut off the stalks of parsley, cilantro, mint and dill, and thinly chop. Put aside.

Heat up 2 Tbsp of olive oil in a pan.

Add in minced onions and brown, then add minced garlic. Mix until soft.

Add diced tomato and sauté in pan until soft.

Add can of tomato paste and thin with a little water

Until mixture is of a smooth, creamy texture and all ingredients have integrated.

Salt and pepper tomato sauce to taste and put aside.

Wash 2 cups of rice. Place in a bowl and add herbs, half of tomato sauce, and all the

Spices except for the cardamom.

Add the other 2 Tbsp of olive oil on top.
Mix together well until all ingredients cohere well together. Salt to taste.
Bring a big pot 2/3 full of water to boil. Add in salt and cumin.
Turn your cabbage head upside down.
Cut a square around the base with its stalk in the center.
Stick a strong knife into its core.
Gently slide the cabbage head into the pot of boiling water,
Using the knife as a handle and allow leaves to steam
Until they begin to part from the cabbage head.
Using a fork, gently nudge leaves that are softening off the cabbage head
And allow to sit in the boiling water for another minute before removing.
Once the removed leaf has cooled, cut the middle stalk out of leaf
by cutting a line on Either side of the stalk.
Save the stalks as you will be lining your pot with them.
Cut the leaf into smaller sections
Spoon some of the rice mixture on to the base of each leaf section.
Make sure the rice forms a line at the base. Try not to overfill each leaf.
Roll edge of cabbage leaf over the rice mixture,
Continue rolling to form little fingers
Continue boiling and releasing cabbage leaves,
Cutting and rolling up sections
Until all your rice mixture is rolled into cabbage leaves.
Add some oil at the bottom of a pot and line with left over cabbage stalks
And/or any leaves you could not roll and feel you can discard.
On top of the stalks, lay your stuffed cabbage rolls in circles, layer upon layer.

Cover your rolls with any remaining stalks/leaves.

Add enough of your chicken/vegetable stock

So that you can see some of the liquid when you nudge aside a few of the rolls.

Throw in cardamom seeds (these should be removed before serving).

Bring your pot to a boil, let boil for 5 minutes,

Then bring down to a simmer and cover with a lid. Allow to cook for 40 minutes.

Check to see if rice is cooked.

Heat up the rest of your tomato sauce.

Place a plate upside down over the pot of cabbage rolls.

Place a steadying hand over the plate and turn over pot

So that your stuffed cabbage rolls remain in formation on the plate.

Gently place on counter and remove pot.

Serve your cabbage rolls hot with the remaining tomato sauce

Egyptian Baked Fish
Ingredients

1 pound fish fillets

4 stalks celery (use only the leaves)

1/2 bunches fresh cilantro (chopped)

1 onions (large, sliced thin and in half)

2 tomatoes (large, chopped)

1 green bell pepper (chopped)

1 red bell pepper (chopped)

1 yellow bell pepper (chopped)

1 jalapeno chilies

3 garlic cloves (fresh, chopped finely or crushed)

1 lemon (large)

1 tablespoon cumin, pepper, salt

3 teaspoons old bay seasoning

1/2 cups unsalted butter (use 1 large stick of butter, not half stick)

Directions

Spray a glass baking dish with a bit of non-stick cooking spray

Or rub lightly with Olive Oil.

Wash the fish well.

Slice the fish into medium size slices.

Lay the fish slices in baking dish.

Sprinkle with cumin, salt, pepper, old bay spice, garlic,

Keep the rest for top later. Squeeze the juice of lemon over this.

Take remaining garlic, jalapeno, celery leaves and cilantro,

Add a half teaspoon of cumin and pound into a paste

Put together and blend well, spread this over fish.

(You can squeeze lemon juice into this to make easier to blend).

Add all chopped vegetables, peppers, onions.

Squeeze the juice of orange into baking dish, top with pats of butter.

Cover with foil and bake in oven at 350 degrees for approximately 45 minutes.

Egyptian Kebabs
Ingredients

Boneless skinless chicken breasts

3 tablespoons yogurt

1⁄4 teaspoon salt, 1⁄4 teaspoon turmeric

1⁄8 teaspoon dry mustard

1⁄2 teaspoon curry powder

1⁄8 teaspoon ground cardamom

1 teaspoon lemon juice, 1 teaspoon white vinegar

1⁄2 small onion, cut in half and broken up into layers

4 small tomatoes, halved

8 bamboo skewers

1 lemon, cut in wedges

DIRECTIONS

Cut chicken breasts into 1 inch cubes, 16 in total.

Combine the yogurt, salt, turmeric, mustard, curry powder,

Cardamom, lemon juice and vinegar in a non-reactive bowl.

Add chicken cubes and let sit in fridge 30-45 minutes.

Soak skewers in water.

Thread chicken, onions and tomatoes onto skewers alternating as follows:

Chicken-onion-chicken-onion-tomato- onion-chicken-onion-chicken-onion.

Grill or broil about 8-10 minutes, turning half way through cooking time.

Garnish with parsley and serve with lemon wedges for squeezing on top.

Egyptian Spinach Soup
Ingredients

1 tablespoon olive oil

1 onion, finely chopped

1⁄4 teaspoon turmeric

4 cups chicken stock, preferably homemade and salt-free

3 -4 scallions, finely chopped

1⁄3 cup basmati rice

Salt and pepper

1 lb spinach (well washed, large stems removed)

2 cups plain yogurt

2 garlic cloves, crushed

DIRECTIONS

Heat the olive oil in a large saucepan and sauté the onion until soft.

Add the turmeric and cook a further minute to let the spice warm through.

Add the stock, scallions, rice, salt and pepper.

Simmer gently for approximately 15 minutes until the rice is cooked.

Do not overcook.

Cut the spinach into chiffonade, add to pan and cook for another five minutes.

To serve hot: Beat yogurt and garlic into the soup,

And reheat gently so the yogurt does not curdle.

To serve cold: Allow soup to cool, add yogurt and garlic and puree.

NOTE

1/4 to 1/2 teaspoon Madras curry powder can be substituted for the turmeric

Depending on how fragrant you want your soup to be.

Egyptian Spiced Prawns
Ingredients

3 tablespoons olive oil

3 garlic cloves, crushed

1 teaspoon paprika

1 teaspoon ground cumin

1 teaspoon ginger, fresh grated

1 1⁄2 lbs large shrimp, raw & shelled

1⁄8 teaspoon sea salt

2 tablespoons fresh coriander, chopped (cilantro)

DIRECTIONS

Heat the oil in a large frying pan; add the garlic and sauté gently for 2-3 minutes.

Add the paprika, cumin and ginger; stir to combine. Stir in prawns,

salt and cilantro. Stir-fry for 5 minutes or until the prawns turn pink.
Serve over hot rice.

Macaroni Béchamel

Ingredients

1 (16 ounce) box penne pasta

2 lbs ground beef

1 medium onion, chopped

2 garlic cloves, minced

2 tablespoons chopped fresh parsley

1 tablespoon fresh thyme

1 teaspoon cinnamon

1 (8 ounce) can tomato sauce

1 beaten egg

1 dash parmesan cheese (optional)

8 cups cold milk

6 tablespoons butter

6 tablespoons flour
1 teaspoon fresh thyme
1⁄2 teaspoon nutmeg (optional)
2 beaten eggs, salt, white and black pepper

DIRECTIONS

Prepare pasta according to directions on the box.

Sauté the onion in a little oil over med high heat until soft.

Add garlic and sauté another 2 minutes.

Add the ground beef and brown.

Drain off the fat, return to the stove

And add the parsley, thyme, and cinnamon until combined.

Stir in the can of tomato sauce and simmer over low heat about 10 minutes.

Remove from the heat and let it cool.

Once it has cooled stir in the beaten egg. Set aside.

TO MAKE THE BACHAMEL SAUCE:

In a large saucepan over med-high heat melt the butter.

Once melted whisk in the flour until smooth. Keep whisking for 2 minute.

Now whisk in the milk slowly until all the milk has been added.

Keep whisking making sure there are no lumps in it.

Add the salt and white and black peppers to your taste.

Whisk pretty continuously until the milk is almost boiling, but not quite.

Now whisk in the thyme and nutmeg (if you want it).

The sauce should now be fairly thick.

Quickly whisk in the beaten eggs. Remove from heat.

TO ASSEMBLE THE DISH:

Mix half the béchamel mixture into the pasta.

Put half the pasta covered with the sauce into a 9x13 baking dish.

Now layer the entire meat mixture over the pasta.

You can top with a sprinkling on Parmesan cheese if you like.

Now add the rest of the Pasta to form the top layer.

Finally, pour and spread the remaining béchamel sauce over the top of the last layer.

Bake it in the oven at 400 degrees for 45-60 min or until the top is golden brown.

Chicken Pane (Breaded Fried Chicken Breasts)
Ingredients

4 boneless skinless chicken breasts

1 lemon, juice of

1 small onion (grated into liquid)

Salt & pepper

1 cup fine breadcrumbs (you may use more or less)
Oil (for frying)

DIRECTIONS

Take and slice your chicken breasts into thinner slices.
Using a sharp knife, and holding one hand on top of breast,
Slice across horizontally giving you a thinner sliced breast.
So one breast should yield about 3 thinner pieces or so
Put slices into glass mixing bowl or dish.
Squeeze the juice of lemon onto chicken slices.
Add the onion liquid
(You can achieve liquid by blending onion in a blender or food processor).
Add salt & pepper and cover with plastic wrap.
Put in refrigerator for at least an hour.
When ready to fry, take a slice and dip into bowl filled with bread crumbs.
Do this until all chicken is breaded, setting each slice on a plate.
Add oil in a large frying pan, enough to cover bottom of each slice.
Fry until golden brown on each side.

Shakshouka

Ingredients

1 large onion (finely chopped)

4 eggs

Cooking oil

6 medium tomatoes

Salt and pepper

DIRECTIONS

In a large frying pan, sauté onion until lightly browned.

Grate tomatoes on largest holes of a grater.

Mix grated tomatoes and onion, cover and cook over low heat for 25 minutes

Remove cover and break eggs over the surface.

Stir gently to break yolks, cover and cook for about 3 or 4 minutes until eggs are set Sprinkle with salt and pepper.

Egyptian Fava Bean Dip

Ingredients

1 1⁄2 cups cooked fava beans

1 small onion, chopped

3 garlic cloves, chopped

1 large tomatoes, chopped

1⁄2 teaspoon chili powder, 1⁄2 teaspoon curry powder

1⁄2 teaspoon cumin (but season to your own taste!)

1 dash cinnamon (but season to your own taste!)

1 dash clove (but season to your own taste!)

1 dash turmeric (but season to your own taste!)

1 dash cayenne (but season to your own taste!)

1 tablespoon lemon juice (or to taste)

Salt

1 small potato, peeled and cooked, added when onion is cooking (optional)

DIRECTIONS

First, cook onion in vegetable oil until limp.

Add garlic and cook a little.

Add large chopped tomato and cook until it just starts breaking apart.

Add spices and lemon juice and stir.

Add fava beans and salt to taste.

Leave on low heat for about 15-20 minutes.

Put in blender and puree until smooth.

Place in serving dish and drizzle generously with olive oil

Optional: add tahini

Eat with Carol's pita bread and salad

Salad

1 onion chopped.

1 cucumber chopped.

1 tomatoes chopped.

1 tablespoon vinegar

Chili powder, cumin, salt to taste

Mix all together.

Beef in Rich Onion Sauce
Ingredients

1 lb stewing beef (you can cut each piece in half if you want)

4 onions (sliced super thin)

2 chicken bouillon cubes

1 bay leaf

2 tablespoons butter

1 tablespoon oil of your choice, but NOT olive oil

Water

Salt & pepper

DIRECTIONS

Wash the meat well.

Put into a saucepan with butter and oil.

Cook until all beef lightly browned.

Add all sliced onions, bouillon cubes, salt and pepper, bay leaf

And stir around cooking on medium-low heat for 15 minutes.

Add water, approximately 1-1/2 cups,

Turn to low, cover and cook for 2 hours or more.

Check during cooking, add more water if too dry.

But the onions should give enough liquid with initial water you added.

When finished you should have super tender beef with a thick oniony sauce.

The onions will have cooked down to a thick rich sauce.

Serve with rice or bread.

Egyptian Koshary
INGREDIENTS

1 cup brown lentils

1 cup basmati rice

1 cup uncooked pasta (small shells or elbow macaroni is best)

2 large onions, diced

4 cloves garlic, minced

2 tablespoons oil

1(400 g) can chopped tomatoes

1/4 teaspoon crushed red chili pepper flakes (or more to taste)

Salt and black pepper

DIRECTIONS

Cook the lentils in just over a litre of salted water.

Bring to a boil, reduce the heat and simmer, covered, for 15-30 minutes,

Depending on the type of lentils you are using.

When the lentils are quite tender, add the rice to the lentils and continue simmering

Until the rice is cooked, adding water if necessary.

Cook the macaroni in a separate pot, Rinse and strain when done.

Meanwhile, fry the onions and garlic in the oil until golden.

Add the tomatoes, chilli flakes, salt and pepper to taste

Let it bubble for 10-20 minutes or until thickened and sauce like.

You can now blitz the sauce in a food processor until smooth or just leave as is.

Mix the lentils, rice and macaroni together in one pot.

Place some of the lentil mixture on each plate and top with tomato sauce.

Sprinkle with more hot chili powder or salt and pepper, if desired.

Egyptian Red Lentil Soup

INGREDIENTS

5 cups vegetable broth or 5 cups water

1 cup dried red lentils

2 cups chopped onions, 2 cups chopped potatoes

8 garlic cloves, peeled and left whole

1 tablespoon canola oil

2 teaspoons ground cumin

1⁄2 teaspoon turmeric, 1 teaspoon salt

1⁄3 cup chopped fresh cilantro

3 tablespoons fresh lemon juice

DIRECTIONS

add the first 5 ingredients to a large pot; cover and bring to a boil.

Lower the heat and simmer 15-20 minutes or until the lentils and veggies are tender.

Take pot from stove burner and set aside.

In a small saucepan, add the oil

Warm over low heat until the oil is hot but not smoking.

Add in the cumin, turmeric, and salt.

Cook and stir constantly for 2-3 minutes or until the cumin has released its fragrance

(Be careful not to scorch the spices).

Set spice mixture aside for 1 minute to cool.

Stir spice mixture into the lentil mixture; add cilantro, stir to combine.

You can puree the soup, in batches, in a blender

OR you can use an immersion blender and blend to desired texture

Add in lemon juice; stir to combine.

Rewarm soup in soup pot; season if needed with salt/pepper.

Egyptian Falafel

INGREDIENTS

250g dried split fava beans, covered in cold water and soaked overnight

3 garlic cloves, crushed

½ leek, finely chopped

5 spring onions, finely chopped

½ tsp bicarbonate of soda

1 tsp gram flour, 1 tbsp. chopped coriander

1 tbsp. chopped parsley, 1 tsp ground cumin

A pinch of cayenne pepper

Salt and black pepper, Sesame seeds Oil for frying

DIRECTIONS

Drain the split fava beans well in a sieve or colander.

Tip them into a food processor, along with the rest of the ingredients, except for the sesame seeds.

Blitz the ingredients to a rough paste and tip it out on to a clean surface.

Divide the mixture into 12-16 pieces, each about the size of a small golf ball.

Press them down with your fingers to make small patties.

Sprinkle around 3 tbsp. sesame seeds on to a plate

And coat each side of the falafels roughly with the seeds.

Transfer them to the fridge for at least 10 minutes.

Fill a small pan with oil to a depth of about 3cm. Heat the oil

it will be ready when a piece of bread dropped in sizzles and turns brown quickly.

Turn the heat down and start to cook the falafel in batches.

. Cook each side for 2-3 minutes,

or until it is golden brown then flip them over and fry the other side.

Serve with a minty yoghurt sauce.

Egypt
ian

Yoghurt Sauce

INGREDIENTS

250ml plain yoghurt

3 tbsp. tahini, 1 garlic clove, crushed

Juice of ½ lemon

Salt and black pepper

2 tbsp. chopped mint

DIRECTIONS

Whisk all the ingredients together

Thin the sauce down to a suitable pouring consistency

With a little cold water.

Baba Ghanoush

INGREDIENTS

1 large eggplant

1 1/2 tablespoons tahini sauce

4 cloves garlic, smashed

1/2 lemon, juiced

1/2 teaspoon red pepper flakes

Salt to taste

1 tablespoon olive oil, or to taste

1 pinch dried parsley flakes, for garnish

DIRECTIONS

Preheat oven to 400 degrees F (200 degrees C).

Arrange oven racks so you have one low and one high in the oven.

Cut a shallow slit along the side of the eggplant and place into a baking dish.

Roast in preheated oven on the lower rack

Until the eggplant is completely shrunken and soft,

. Move dish to higher rack and continue baking until the skin is charred

. Let eggplant cool until cool enough to handle.

Peel and discard skin from eggplant.

Put eggplant into a bowl; add tahini, garlic, lemon juice,

Red pepper flakes, and salt.

Stir until ingredients are evenly mixed.

Drizzle olive oil over the baba ghanoush and garnish with parsley.

Tomato Salad

Ingredients:

3 to 4 large vine-ripened tomatoes, sliced 1/4-inch thick

5 to 6 cloves garlic, minced

Juice and zest of 1 lemon

4 tablespoons extra-virgin olive oil

4 tablespoons white vinegar

1 teaspoon sea salt

1 teaspoon coarsely-ground black pepper

1 teaspoon cumin powder

1/4 cup fresh parsley, chopped

1/4 cup fresh cilantro, chopped

Arugula leaves, washed and trimmed or 1 bag of arugula

1/4 cup extra-virgin olive oil

DIRECTIONS

In a small bowl, mix together the garlic, lemon juice, lemon zest,

Olive oil, vinegar, salt, black pepper, cumin, parsley, and cilantro; set aside.

In a deep dish with a lip, arrange sliced tomatoes over the bottom of the dish.

Pour the prepared dressing over the tomatoes.

Cover tomato and dressing with plastic wrap

And let sit in the refrigerator for a couple hours

For the flavours to marinate with the tomatoes.

Halfway through, turn the tomatoes once to coat well on both sides.

Approximately 20 minutes before ready to serve,

Spread the arugula on a serving platter

And arrange the tomato slices on the arugula with all the juices

and herbs from the dressing.

Garnish with additional fresh chopped parsley and cilantro.

Serve salad at room temperature for best flavour.

Egyptian Salad

INGREDIENTS

1 green sweet pepper

1 onion, 1 tomato

1 mini (Lebanese) cucumber

Some butter head lettuce leaves (eg: Salanova)

DRESSING INGREDIENTS

Garlic, 1 spoon of fine cut coriander

1 spoon of lemon juice

2 spoons of olive oil, Salt and pepper

DIRECTIONS

Cut and mix all ingredients. Serve in a big bowl to share

Potato Salad

INGREDIENTS

5 potatoes, cooked, peeled and diced into ½ inch cubes

2 hardboiled eggs, peeled and chopped.

¼ cup chopped green onions, ¼ cup chopped parsley

2 tablespoons chopped fresh mint

¼ cup olive oil, 2 cloves garlic

¼ cup lemon juice, Salt & pepper to taste

DIRECTIONS

Place the first six ingredients in a large salad bowl.

In a separate bowl, mash the garlic with the salt, then add the lemon juice &

.Add the dressing to the rest of the ingredients and toss gently, being careful not to crumble the potatoes and the eggs, Serve chilled.

Green Beans, Black-Eyed Peas Salad

INGREDIENTS

16 ounce bag frozen French cut green beans

16 ounce can black-eyed peas

2 large ripe tomatoes, chopped

½ cup(s) chopped parsley

4 scallions, chopped

Juice of 2 lemons

1 tablespoon vegetable oil

DIRECTIONS

Steam and drain the green beans and allow them to cool completely.

Drain and rinse the black eyed peas.

Combine all ingredients and mix well.

May be served chilled.